MODERN BAND METHOD

Guitar

Book 1

Scott Burstein
Spencer Hale
Mary Claxton
Dave Wish

Contributors:
Tony Sauza, Clayton McIntyre, Lauren Brown, Joe Panganiban

To access audio and video visit:
www.halleonard.com/mylibrary

Enter Code
6925-5193-4424-5976

ISBN 978-1-5400-7668-7

Visit Hal Leonard Online at
www.halleonard.com

Contact us:
Hal Leonard
7777 West Bluemound Road
Milwaukee, WI 53213
Email: info@halleonard.com

In Europe, contact:
Hal Leonard Europe Limited
1 Red Place
London, W1K 6PL
Email: info@halleonardeurope.com

In Australia, contact:
Hal Leonard Australia Pty. Ltd.
4 Lentara Court
Cheltenham, Victoria, 3192 Australia
Email: info@halleonard.com.au

Introduction

Welcome!

If you are reading this, you have already made the decision to learn to play guitar so you can play some of your favorite songs. One of the best things about playing in a Modern Band is that you don't need much time to start jammin', but there are plenty of skills to learn and master over time too. Most popular musicians are able to perform in a wide variety of musical styles by playing chords with different rhythms to accompany a vocalist. They often add memorable riffs, or short melodic phrases, that stay in your head all day. This method book is designed to teach you skills to play guitar and create music in a variety of popular music styles—pop, rock, R&B, funk, hip-hop, and more. Let's get started!

Jam Tracks 🔊 and Video Lessons ▶

Use the audio Jam Tracks throughout this book to practice the songs and exercises. Also be sure to watch the included video lessons that demonstrate many of the techniques and concepts. To access all of the audio and video files for download or streaming, just visit *www.halleonard.com/mylibrary* and enter the code found on page 1 of this book.

Parts of the Guitar

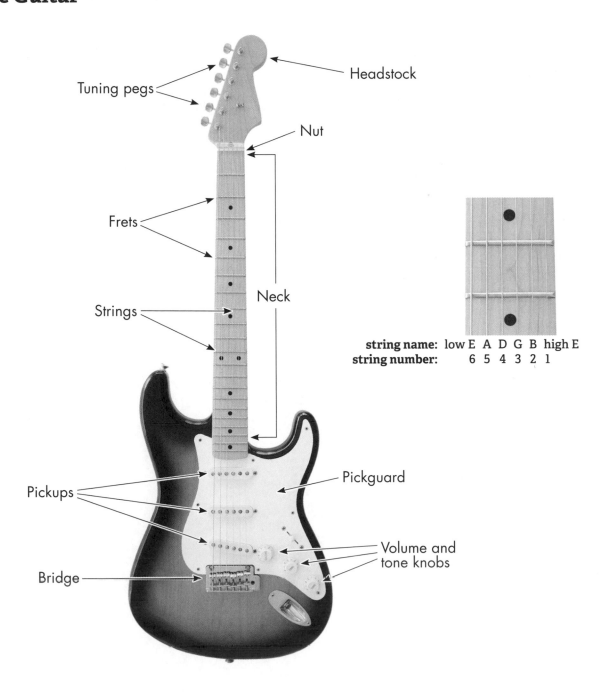

string name: low E A D G B high E
string number: 6 5 4 3 2 1

Tuning ▶

Even if you're using perfect technique, your guitar won't sound right if it's not in tune. Be sure to watch the video and tune your guitar before you start playing.

Basic Technique ▶

If you're playing a right-handed guitar, hold the neck of the guitar in your left hand and rest the body of the guitar on your lap. If you're standing, you should use a strap to hold the instrument and adjust it to a comfortable height. If you're using a left-handed instrument, use the opposite hands.

You play notes by strumming or plucking the strings with a guitar pick.

Hold the pick between your thumb and index finger. Grip near the tip of the pick so that you will have more control, but not so close that your fingers are hitting the strings. Then strum through all the strings up and down.

Notation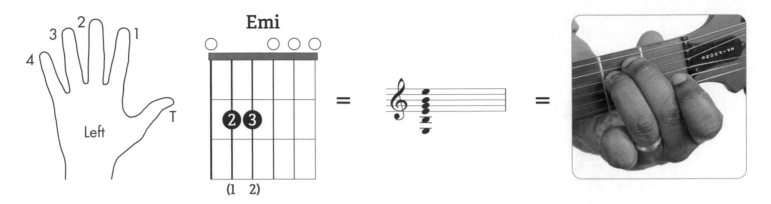

Here are a few graphics that will show up throughout each section. The first is the **chord diagram**. The numbers refer to the left-hand fingers used to press down the strings (for a right-handed guitar player). The open circles tell you to play a string **open**, or without holding down any frets. If you see an "X" over a string, it means to not play that string.

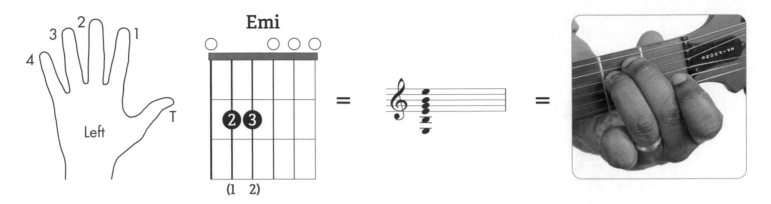

Strumming

Next, let's look at how we notate rhythms. Count these numbers steadily, "1, 2, 3, 4, 1, 2, 3, 4...," and strum down on the black numbers. Strumming on the numbers is called playing the "on-beats."

1	2	3	4

1	2	3	4

The "+" signs (spoken as "and") between numbers are called "off-beats." When playing these, strum up through the strings rather than down.

1	2	3 + 4

1 + 2 + 3	4

Learning rhythms and chords will improve your ability to "comp." **Comping** means using your musical knowledge to make up rhythms over a chord progression that fit a song's style.

This book is designed for you to learn alongside other Modern Band musicians so you can jam with your friends and classmates, but it can also be used as a stand-alone book to learn to play guitar. Though some of the skills that you will be working on during each section will be different from those of the other instruments, all of the Full Band Songs are designed to be played by a whole band together. Now, let's start playing some music!

Playing Chords: One-Chord Jam

Play the easy E minor chord (Emi) using the rhythms shown below. You don't have to put any fingers on the fretboard for this one… just strum the three open strings.

Easy Emi

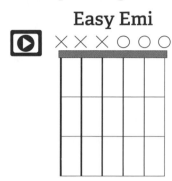

Count to four and strum down ( ) on every black beat. Don't play the grey beats.

1	2	3	4

1	2	3	4

1	2	3	4

Now try these strum patterns with two more chords.

 Easy G

 Easy C

Improvisation: Two-Note Solo

The two notes shown here can be used to take a solo—the open 1st string, which is the note E, and the 3rd fret on the 1st string, which is the note G. Unlike the chord diagrams, this image shows two notes that you can play on the guitar, but not at the same time.

Practice playing these two notes in a variety of ways by mixing up the rhythm and order. Here are some ideas for improvisation:

- Start by playing the open note twice and switching to the G.
- Alternate between the two notes rapidly and then slowly. Then try changing speeds.
- Focus on rhythm and lock in with the Jam Track.
- Play a rhythm on just the E, and then repeat that rhythm on the G.

Music Theory: The Song Chart ▶

One way music is written is with a **lead sheet**. A lead sheet tells a musician how to play the chords of a song. The lead sheet example below has four **measures** (or **bars**), which are divided by vertical lines (**bar lines**). Each measure is made up of four beats, shown by the diagonal lines, or **slashes** (/). You can play any four-beat strum patterns over those four beats. The measures are repeated over and over again, indicated by the **repeat bar**.

The next part of the lead sheet is the chords. The song below uses a G chord for four beats (one measure), then an Emi chord for four beats, a C chord for four beats, and finally another Emi chord for four beats.

CAN'T STOP THE FEELING! 🔊
Justin Timberlake

Another way music is written is with the names of the chords over the song lyrics. This type of chart doesn't tell you how many beats to play each chord, but it shows you which lyrics you sing when the chords change. Play G when you sing "feeling" and switch to Emi on the word "bones."

        G   Emi

I've got this feeling inside my bones.

    C   Emi

It goes electric, wavy when I turn it on.

      G   Emi

All through my city, all through my home,

    C   Emi

We're flying up, no ceiling, when we in our zone.

     G   Emi

I got that sunshine in my pocket, got that good soul in my feet.

    C   Emi

I feel that hot blood in my body when it drops, ooh.

     G   Emi

I can't take my eyes up off it, moving so phenomenally.

    C   Emi

Room on lock the way we rock it, so don't stop.

Here are some other songs that use the same three chords, Emi, G, and C. In the first two songs, each chord is played for eight beats.

WITHOUT YOU 🔊

David Guetta ft. Usher

Easy G   Easy C   Easy Emi   Easy C

```
|: / / / / | / / / / | / / / / | / / / / | / / / / | / / / / | / / / / | / / / / :|
```

```
⊓   ⊓   ⊓   ⊓
1   2   3   4
```

G   **C**   **Emi**   **C**
I can't win, I can't reign. I will never win this game without you, without you.

G   **C**   **Emi**   **C**
I am lost, I am vain. I will never be the same without you, without you.

G   **C**   **Emi**   **C**
I won't run, I won't fly. I will never make it by without you, without you.

G   **C**   **Emi**   **C**
I can't rest, I can't fight. All I need is you and I, without you, without you.

SEND MY LOVE (TO YOUR NEW LOVER) 🔊

Adele

Easy G   Easy Emi

```
|: / / / / | / / / / | / / / / | / / / / :|
```

```
⊓   ⊓   ⊓   ⊓
1   2   3   4
```

G   **Emi**
This was all you, none of it me. You put your hands on, on my body and told me,
     you told me you were ready

G   **Emi**
For the big one, for the big jump. I'd be your last love, everlasting, you and me.
     That was what you told me.

G   **Emi**
I'm giving you up, I've forgiven it all. You set me free.

G
Send my love to your new lover, treat her better.

     Emi
We've gotta let go of all of our ghosts. We both know we ain't kids no more.

G
Send my love to your new lover, treat her better.

     Emi
We've gotta let go of all of our ghosts.
     We both know we ain't kids no more.

In this song, the Emi and C chords are played for two beats each, and then G is played for four beats.

WAKE ME UP

Avicii ft. John Legend

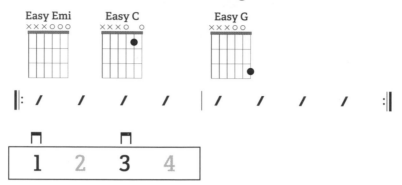

Emi   **C**   **G**
Feeling my way through the darkness,

Emi   **C**   **G**
Guided by a beating heart.

Emi   **C**   **G**
I can't tell where the journey will end,

Emi   **C**   **G**
But I know where to start.

Emi   **C**   **G**
They tell me I'm too young to understand.

Emi   **C**   **G**
They say I'm caught up in a dream.

Emi   **C**   **G**
Well, life will pass me by if I don't open up my eyes.

Emi   **C**   **G**
Well, that's fine by me.

Emi   **C**   **G**
So wake me up when it's all over,

Emi   **C**   **G**
When I'm wiser and I'm older.

Emi   **C**   **G**
All this time I was finding myself

Emi   **C**   **G**
And I didn't know I was lost.

Composition: Emi, G, C

Use the Emi, G, and C chords to create your own song. Place the chords in the song chart below in any order you'd like. Then, pick one of the strumming patterns to play those chords.

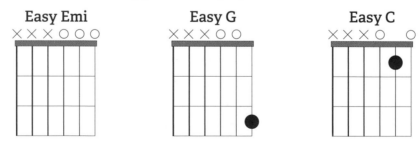

Chords:

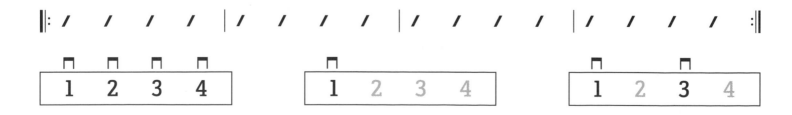

Full Band Song: I GOTTA FEELING

The Black Eyed Peas

Form of Recording: Intro–Chorus–Verse–Chorus–Verse–Chorus

Easy G
××××○○

Easy C
××××○ ○

Easy Emi
×××○○○

Easy C
××××○ ○

‖: ∕ ∕ ∕ ∕ | ∕ ∕ ∕ ∕ | ∕ ∕ ∕ ∕ | ∕ ∕ ∕ ∕ | ∕ ∕ ∕ ∕ | ∕ ∕ ∕ ∕ | ∕ ∕ ∕ ∕ | ∕ ∕ ∕ ∕ :‖

Use this rhythm for the Chorus:

⊓   ⊓   ⊓   ⊓
| 1 | 2 | 3 | 4 |

And use this rhythm for the Verse
(V means to strum up):

⊓ V ⊓ V ⊓ V ⊓ V
| 1 + 2 + 3 + 4 + |

CHORUS
     G   C
I gotta feeling that tonight's gonna be a good night,

               Emi   C
That tonight's gonna be a good night, that tonight's gonna be a good, good night.

VERSE
G   C
Tonight's the night, let's live it up. I got my money, let's spend it up.

Emi   C
Go out and smash it, like, oh my God. Jump off that sofa, let's get, get off.

VERSE
G   C
I know that we'll have a ball if we get down and go out and just lose it all.

     Emi   C
I feel stressed out, I wanna let go. Let's go way out, spaced out, and losing all control.

VERSE
G   C
Fill up my cup, Mazel Tov! Look at her dancing, just take it off.

Emi
Let's paint the town, we'll shut it down.
   C
Let's burn the roof, and then we'll do it again.

Going Beyond: Singing and Playing

An important skill for a popular musician is to not only play songs, but also to sing along. Here are a few tips for singing and playing:

- Make sure you have learned the guitar part well enough to play it without thinking about changing chords, then try speaking the lyrics in rhythm over it.
- Sing the lyrics while fretting the chords with just the left hand. Strum only when it's time to change chords.
- Don't worry too much about singing the correct pitches (notes) at this point; just practice the skill of doing two things at once.

SECTION 2

Playing Chords: One-Chord Song

Play the new chord A and use the strumming pattern below to play "Low Rider" by War. Make sure you strum down on the beats (⊓) and up on the "+" symbols (V).

You can also practice a different two-note solo. In the diagram below, a fret ("fr") number is given as a reference.

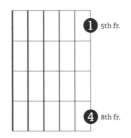

Music Theory: Reading Guitar Tab

Tablature is another way to write music. It is used to write melodies and riffs. The tab staff has six lines and each line represents a string. The thickest string on the guitar is the lowest line on the tab.

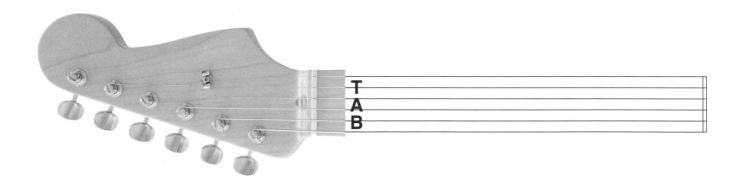

"Dark Horse" by Katy Perry has a riff played on the two thinnest strings of the guitar: strings 1 and 2. The numbers on the string tell us which fret to push down. For now, listen to the original song to get a sense of the rhythm to play.

DARK HORSE
Katy Perry

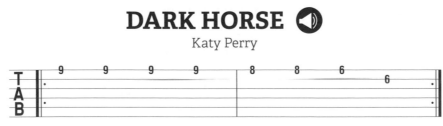

This next riff is played on the lowest string of the guitar:

25 OR 6 TO 4
Chicago

Instrument Technique: Strengthening Your Fingers

Tablature is also useful for notating exercises. Try the exercise below for moving between fingers 1 and 2. Repeat this exercise with different fingers and on different frets.

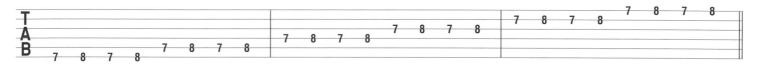

Playing Chords: Easy Ami

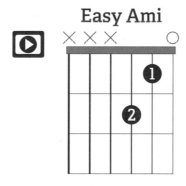

Easy Ami

The easy A minor chord (Ami) uses two fingers and is similar to the C chord. Try switching between the two chords with the song "Shout" by the Isley Brothers. Keep your pointer finger on the 1st fret of the 2nd string to make switching between these chords simple and smooth.

SHOUT
The Isley Brothers

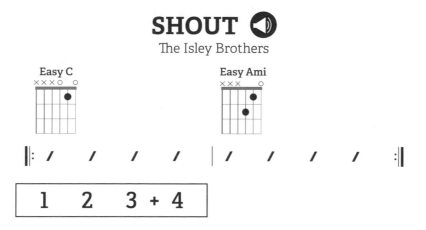

Playing Chords: Easy E

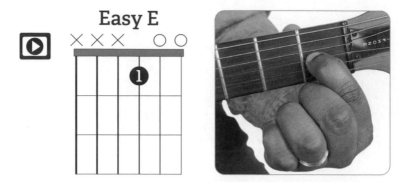

You can change between the C and E chord by moving your first finger up or down one string.

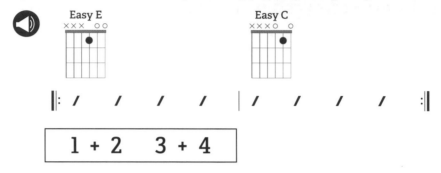

Improvisation: Four-Note Solo

You can expand the two-note solo to four notes by playing the same frets on the next string. Try improvising using these four notes. Another musician can play the Ami chord along with you and the Jam Track.

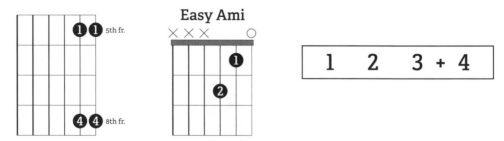

Music Theory: Whole Notes and Half Notes

In each measure of music so far, you have counted four beats. If you strum a chord once and let it ring for four beats, it lasts the whole measure. That is called a **whole note**. If it is cut in half, it becomes two **half notes**. Each whole note is four beats long and each half note is two beats long.

Below, whole and half notes in traditional notation are shown along with strumming notation.

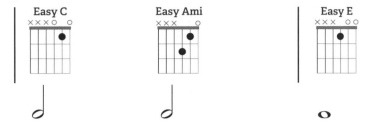

Twenty One Pilots

Form of Recording: Chorus–Verse–Chorus–Verse–Chorus–Chorus

Using traditional notation and chord diagrams, you can read and play the Chorus of "Heathens" by Twenty One Pilots.

Below is the full song shown with slashes and chord diagrams, as well as the chord and lyric chart. In addition to the full Jam Track for this song, there are also two separate Jam Tracks for the Chorus and Verse looped so you can practice them individually.

Notice that the Verse includes some different chords that you already know, but played on different beats than the Chorus pattern. The final B "chord" is something new. For now, just play the one note as shown.

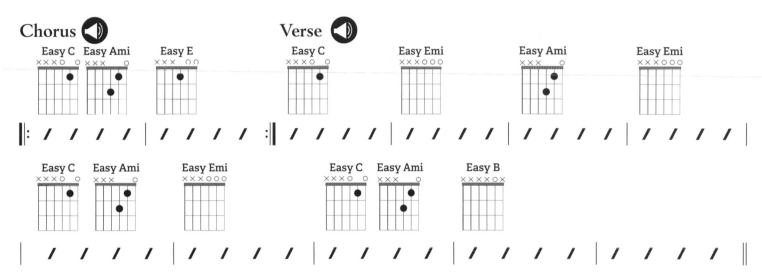

CHORUS

C   Ami   E   C   Ami   E
All my friends are heathens, take it slow. Wait for them to ask you who you know.

     C   Ami   E   C   Ami   E
Please don't make any sudden moves. You don't know the half of the abuse.

VERSE

C
Welcome to the room of people who have rooms of people
       Emi
       that they loved one day docked away.

Ami
Just because we check the guns at the door doesn't mean
       Emi
       our brains will change from hand grenades.

C   Ami   Emi
You'll never know the psychopath sitting next to you.
       You'll never know the murderer sitting next to you.

C   Ami   B
You'll think, "How'd I get here, sitting next to you?"
       But after all I've said, please don't forget.

Words and Music by Tyler Joseph
© 2016 WARNER-TAMERLANE PUBLISHING CORP. and STRYKER JOSEPH MUSIC
All Rights Administered by WARNER-TAMERLANE PUBLISHING CORP.
All Rights Reserved Used by Permission

SECTION 3

Instrument Technique: Chromatic Riffs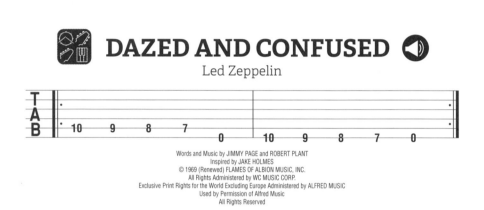

In this next tab example, use a different finger to play each different fret. When we move like this from one fret to the next in an upward or downward line, it is called **chromatic**. If you need to, you can move your hand up and down on the neck.

```
T
A   7  8  9  10   7  8  9  10   7  8  9  10   7  8  9  10   7  8  9  10   7  8  9  10
B   7  8  9  10
```

```
T   10 9  8  7   10 9  8  7   10 9  8  7   10 9  8  7
A              10 9  8  7              10 9  8  7
B                         10 9  8  7
```

Now, check out your chromatic skills with this heavy Led Zeppelin riff. Listen to the original recording to hear the rhythms.

DAZED AND CONFUSED
Led Zeppelin

```
T
A
B   10  9  8  7        10  9  8  7  0
              0
```

Playing Chords: D

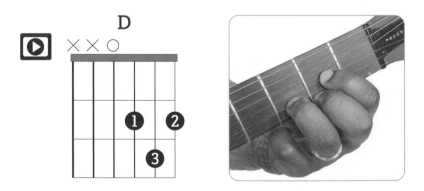

Using the D and A chords, you can play a variety of songs.

IMAGINE 🔊
John Lennon

A
D   A   D
Imagine there's no heaven. It's easy if you try.

A
D   A   D
No hell below us. Above us only sky.

A
D   A   D
Imagine there's no countries. It isn't hard to do.

A
D   A   D
Nothing to kill or die for, and no religion, too.

BEST DAY OF MY LIFE 🔊
American Authors

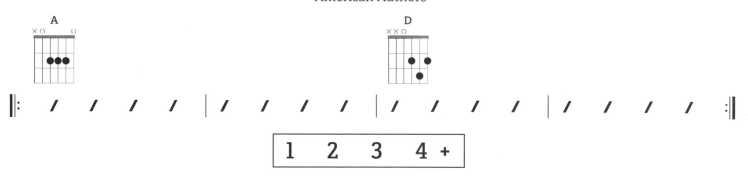

A
I had a dream so big and loud. I jumped so high I touched the clouds.

D
Whoa-o-o-o-o-oh. Whoa-o-o-o-o-oh.

A
I stretched my hands out to the sky. We danced with monsters through the night.

D
Whoa-o-o-o-o-oh. Whoa-o-o-o-o-oh.

A   D
Woo-o-o-o-oo! This is gonna be the best day of my life, my life.

A   D
Woo-o-o-o-oo! This is gonna be the best day of my life, my life.

Music Theory: Quarter and Eighth Notes

Half notes can be broken into two **quarter notes**. Each quarter note gets one beat.

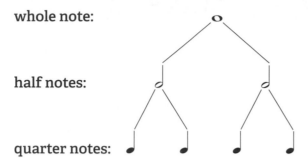

Playing and Resting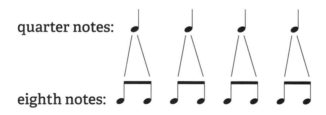

You can also use a **rest** when you want to stop the strings from ringing and leave some space. Try this with the A chord. A rest means "count, but don't play." Each **quarter rest** gets one beat.

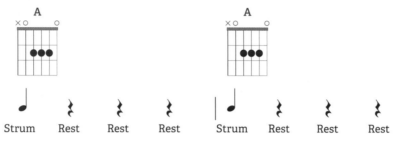

This strumming pattern is useful to practice changing chords.

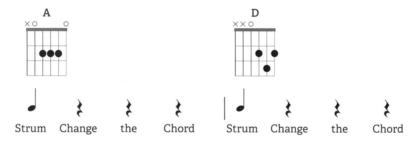

Quarter notes can be broken into **eighth notes**. Each eighth note gets a half of a beat.

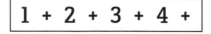

This rhythm:

1 + 2 + 3 + 4 +

...is just eight eighth notes:

These strum patterns use quarter and eighth notes in different combinations. Try strumming and counting them.

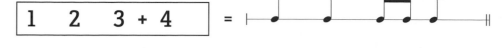

Improvisation: Six-Note Solo

You can add two more notes to the four-note solo to make a six-note solo. In order to play along with the past two Jam Tracks, move your first finger down to fret 2. Use the previous two songs to practice this solo!

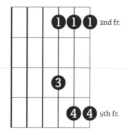

Composition: Compose a Riff

Using the notes in the six-note solo, create your own riff. Here are a few sample riffs:

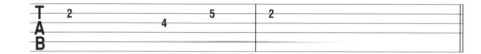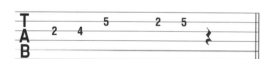

Write your original riff here:

You can play your composed riff over the A to D chord progression. Here are some new strumming patterns you can use:

```
1 + 2   3 + 4          1   2   3 + 4
```

Instrument Technique: Some New Riffs

Listen to the following songs to get a sense of the rhythms. In this first riff, focus on changing strings and alternating the pick up and down in the fast part:

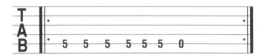

UNDER PRESSURE
Queen ft. David Bowie

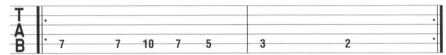

Practice this next riff using different finger combinations, or even just using your first finger the whole time.

SEVEN NATION ARMY
The White Stripes

Playing Chords: Full E

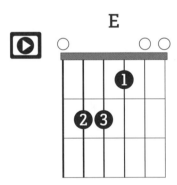

Try the full open E chord with this song:

WE WILL ROCK YOU
Queen

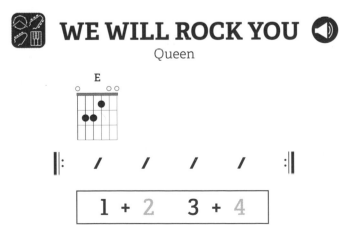

The next two songs have a variety of strum patterns to choose from. Some require you to play an up strum without playing a down strum. To do this, keep the up-and-down motion of your arm going, but just miss the strings on the way down. These patterns, in which upbeats are played after skipping downbeats, are called **syncopated** rhythms.

BACK IN BLACK
AC/DC

Here are several strum patterns you can use for this song, from most basic to most complex:

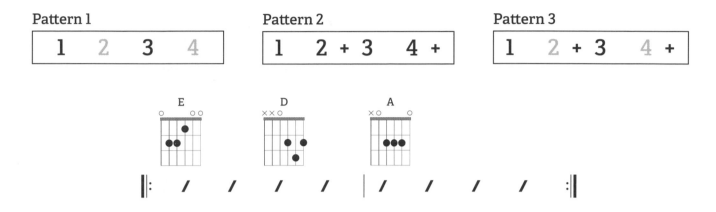

Pattern 1 — 1 2 3 4
Pattern 2 — 1 2 + 3 4 +
Pattern 3 — 1 2 + 3 4 +

E   D   A

WHAT MAKES YOU BEAUTIFUL
One Direction

Here again are several strum patterns you can use for this song:

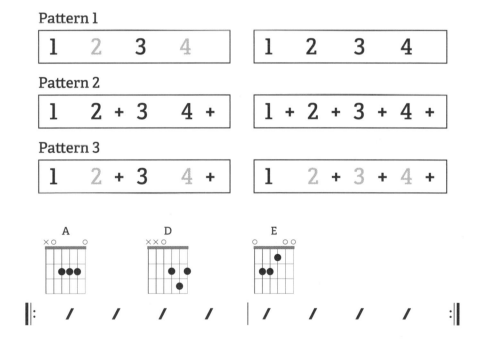

Pattern 1 — 1 2 3 4 | 1 2 3 4
Pattern 2 — 1 2 + 3 4 + | 1 + 2 + 3 + 4 +
Pattern 3 — 1 2 + 3 4 + | 1 2 + 3 + 4 +

A   D   E

Composition: Writing Lyrics

Here are three steps you can take to write your own song lyrics:

1. Pick a theme. Lyrics can be easy to write when you have something you want to say. Think of something you care about and write based on that, such as friends, family, hobbies, or dreams.

2. Choose two words that rhyme, such as "great" and "late," or "thrill" and "chill." Then, choose another pair.

3. Turn your words into sentences. Try to speak the words in rhythm and sing them with the Jam Track. Here is an example of a verse for a song written about songwriting:

Writing	lyrics	is	so	fun,		can	be	done	by	any	-	one.
/	/	/	/			/	/	/		/		/

Think	of	what	to	write	a -	bout;		play	some	chords,	and	sing	or	shout!
/	/	/	/					/	/	/		/		/

Full Band Song: STIR IT UP
Bob Marley & the Wailers

Form of Recording: Intro–Chorus–Verse–Chorus–Verse–Chorus

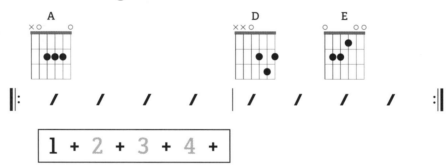

CHORUS

A   D   E   A   D   E
Stir it up. Little darlin', stir it up. Come on, baby.

                    A   D   E   A   D   E
Come on and stir it up. Little darlin', stir it up. O-oh!

VERSE

    A   D
It's been a long, long time, yeah (stir it, stir it, stir it together).

E   A   D   E
Since I got you on my mind (ooh-ooh-ooh-ooh).

A   D   E
Now you are here (stir it, stir it, stir it together). I said, it's so clear.

    A   D   E
To see what we could do, baby (ooh-ooh-ooh-ooh). Just me and you.

SECTION 5

Instrument Technique: Hammer-Ons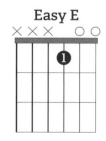

To play a **hammer-on**, pick the first note and then hammer your fret-hand fingertip down on the next note to create the sound without picking it. Here are some examples. Try them with different finger combinations. The curved line over the hammer-ons is called a **slur**, which tells you not to pick the second note.

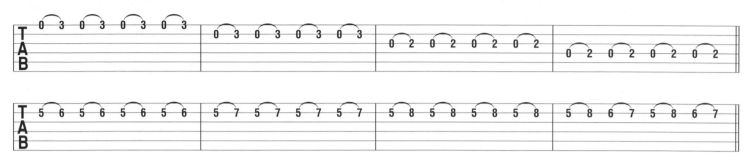

You can add hammer-ons into melodies you've already played:

You can play that same melody on a different set of strings and frets. Is it easier to play hammer-ons with open strings or with fretted notes?

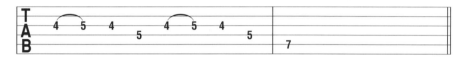

You can do multiple hammer-ons in a row as well, like in this song:

AM I EVIL?

Metallica

Music Theory: Notes, Chords, and Scales

All music is made up of the notes of the musical alphabet. All the riffs and chords you have been playing are made up of these individual notes. There are seven **natural notes**: A–B–C–D–E–F–G.

Chords are a combination of notes played together. For instance, the easy E chord has three different notes in it, while the full E chord has six.

A **scale** is a series of notes. The notes we've been using for soloing are an example of a scale. Below is a sample scale that we will learn more about later in the book.

The combination of notes, chords, and scales put to rhythm defines all the music we experience.

Instrument Technique: Alternate Picking ▶

Just as you can strum up and down, you can pick single strings up and down. Alternate up and down picking on the next two exercises.

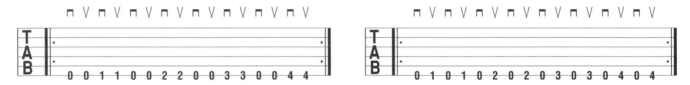

You can also use this exercise to practice hammer-ons. In this case, just use down picks:

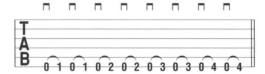

Here is a riff example that uses alternate picking:

MISERLOU 🔊
Dick Dale

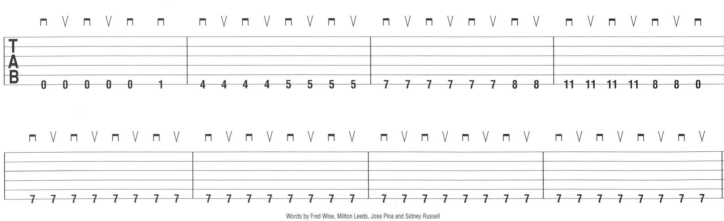

Now, try creating your own riff using alternate picking:

Improvisation: Minor Pentatonic Scale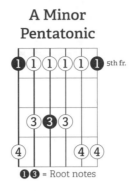

The first scale you'll learn is the **minor pentatonic scale**. The six-note solo from earlier can be expanded to cover all the strings.

A Minor Pentatonic

The **tonic**, or **root**, is the note a scale or chord is named after. For this scale, starting at the 5th fret on string 6, the tonic is A. All the darkened notes in the diagram are A notes.

This scale sounds good with songs that have a bluesy or funky sound, like "Low Rider" by War.

One way to practice this scale is to play it using hammer-ons:

Here are a few riffs that use the pentatonic scale. Note the use of hammer-ons in a few measures.

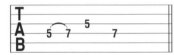  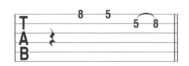 

Try to make some of your own riffs with the minor pentatonic scale:

Playing Chords: One-Chord Song

Here's a song that uses just one chord. You can practice with either a recording of the song or with your whole band.

 # LAND OF A THOUSAND DANCES

Wilson Pickett

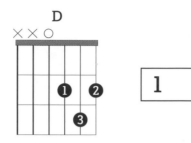

Instrument Technique: Pull-Offs

A **pull-off** is the opposite of a hammer-on. Instead of creating sound by hammering a finger down on the fretboard, create it by pulling a finger off. To get a full sound, you need to pull the finger downward off of the string, as opposed to just lifting it off.

Here are some riffs with pull-offs to open strings.

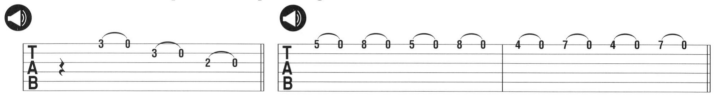

When pulling off to another fretted finger, be sure to keep the fretted finger held in place. Practice with the A minor pentatonic scale.

Improvisation: Applying Hammer-Ons and Pull-Offs

Try including hammer-ons and pull-offs in your improvisation. When using these techniques, make sure that the second note is as loud as the first. Here are some sample riffs.

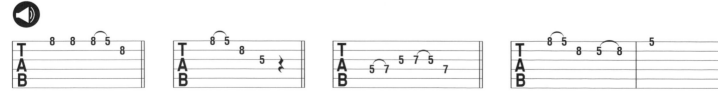

Music Theory: The Music Staff

Look at this melody from a song you have already learned, "Heathens" by Twenty One Pilots. This is the vocal melody written in tablature:

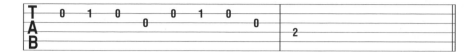

Words and Music by Tyler Joseph
© 2016 WARNER-TAMERLANE PUBLISHING CORP. and STRYKER JOSEPH MUSIC
All Rights Administered by WARNER-TAMERLANE PUBLISHING CORP.
All Rights Reserved Used by Permission

Every note on the guitar has a place on the **music staff**. To start, look at a music staff, which is similar to a tab staff but with a few differences—there are five lines instead of six, and the lines *do not* refer to strings.

The next important feature on a staff is the **treble clef**. It assigns specific note names to the lines and spaces on the staff.

You have already seen note heads used with rhythms. Here they are placed on the staff in the lines and spaces to let the musician know which notes to play. The vertical placement of each note determines what note it is. Here is the same vocal melody in both tab and staff notation.

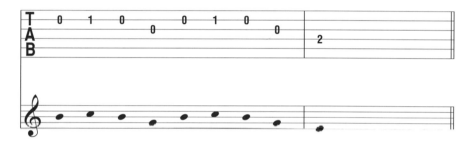

Finally, add the rhythms you learned earlier to the note heads on the staff. In the case of this song, there is a full measure of eighth notes followed by a whole note. Here, the eighth notes are beamed in groups of four instead of two.

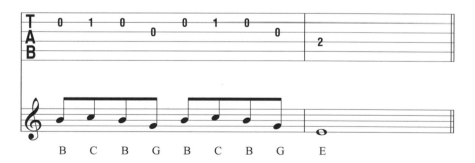

Each note is named by one of the seven (natural) letters of the musical alphabet. For now, look at the notes on the first three frets of the guitar and on the first four strings. Notice that the staves are switched this time. In guitar music, the tab staff is usually shown on the bottom.

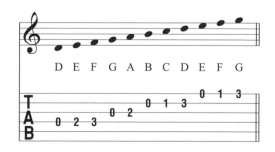

27

For the song below, write the notes of the tab numbers in the bottom staff for the first two measures. Then, write the tab numbers in the top staff for the notes shown in measures 3–5. We have slightly changed the rhythm so it uses only the note values we have discussed so far.

BAD ROMANCE
Lady Gaga

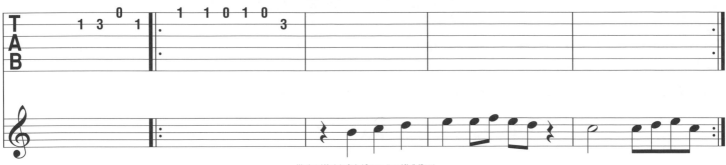

Now, try playing your example, reading the staff notation and then the tab.

> From this point on, standard staff notation will be included with the tabs. Use this to begin familiarizing yourself with where the notes are on the staff. If you see any symbols or rhythms you don't understand, continue listening to the original recordings to hear the rhythms. You'll learn more about music reading as you continue through the Modern Band program.

To play the next melody from "Bad Romance," we'll need to know the **eighth rest**: ⁊. This rest takes the place of one eighth note. Combined with another eighth note or eighth rest, it makes up a full beat. Find a recording of this song and listen to the melody to hear how the rhythm works with the notation. This melody happens at the 0:29 mark on the original recording.

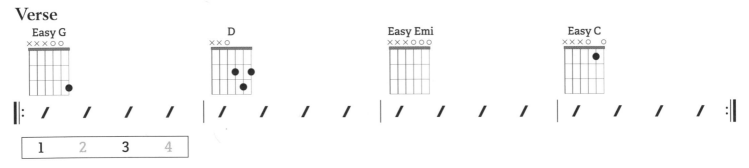

Full Band Song: SOMEONE LIKE YOU
Adele

Form of Recording: Intro–Verse–Pre-Chorus–Chorus–Verse–Pre-Chorus–Chorus–Bridge–Chorus

Verse

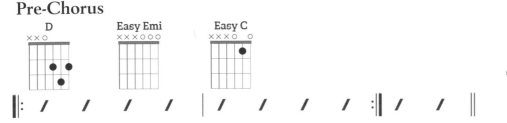

Pre-Chorus

Chorus

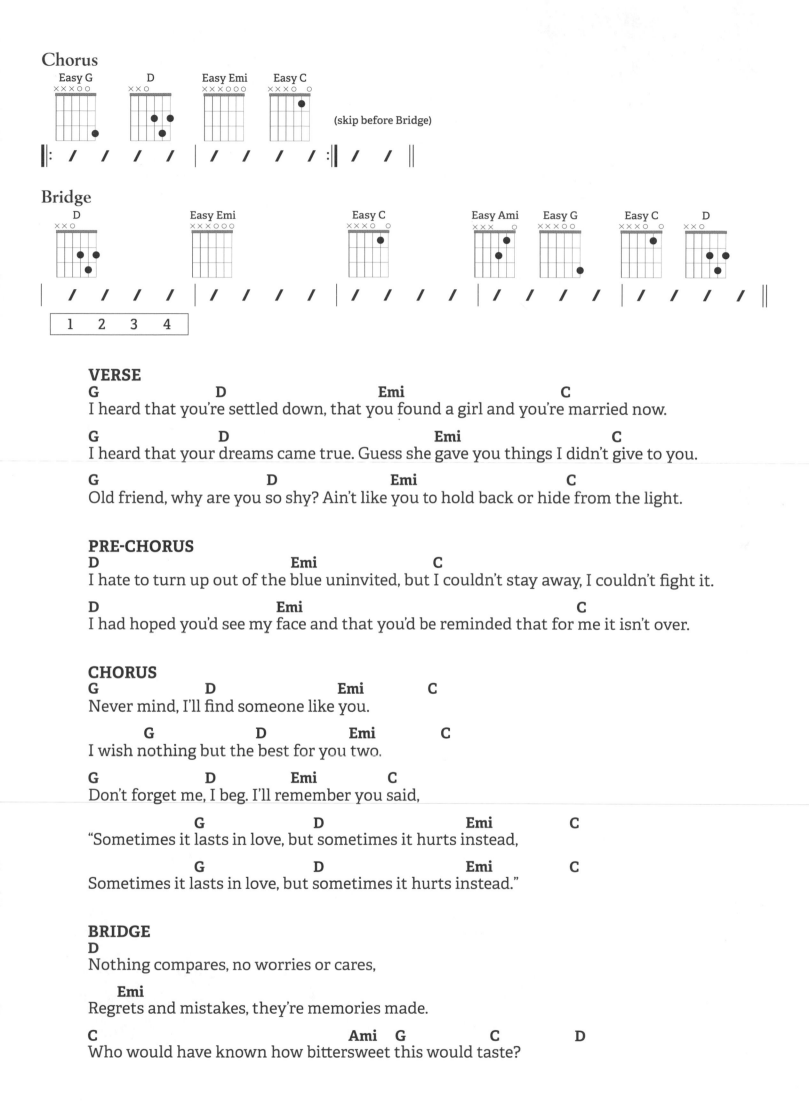

Easy G · D · Easy Emi · Easy C (skip before Bridge)

Bridge

D · Easy Emi · Easy C · Easy Ami · Easy G · Easy C · D

1 2 3 4

VERSE

G   D   Emi   C
I heard that you're settled down, that you found a girl and you're married now.

G   D   Emi   C
I heard that your dreams came true. Guess she gave you things I didn't give to you.

G   D   Emi   C
Old friend, why are you so shy? Ain't like you to hold back or hide from the light.

PRE-CHORUS

D   Emi   C
I hate to turn up out of the blue uninvited, but I couldn't stay away, I couldn't fight it.

D   Emi   C
I had hoped you'd see my face and that you'd be reminded that for me it isn't over.

CHORUS

G   D   Emi   C
Never mind, I'll find someone like you.

               G   D   Emi   C
I wish nothing but the best for you two.

G   D   Emi   C
Don't forget me, I beg. I'll remember you said,

               G   D   Emi   C
"Sometimes it lasts in love, but sometimes it hurts instead,

               G   D   Emi   C
Sometimes it lasts in love, but sometimes it hurts instead."

BRIDGE

D
Nothing compares, no worries or cares,

    Emi
Regrets and mistakes, they're memories made.

C   Ami G   C   D
Who would have known how bittersweet this would taste?

Playing Chords: Strumming Patterns

Practice playing through these patterns while staying on the same chord of your choice.

1 2 3 4	1 2 3 4	1 + 2 + 3 + 4 +

1 2 + 3 + 4 +	1 2 + 3 + 4	1 + 2 + 3 + 4 +

Composition: Introduction

A lot of songs have an **introduction** (or intro). An introduction is often the instrumental section that happens before the vocalist begins. To compose an introduction, write four bars using the chords you know, and be sure to use at least one minor chord. Use the Jam Track to try out your ideas.

Chords:

‖: / / / / | / / / / | / / / / | / / / / :‖

Strumming Pattern:

Now add a riff to your introduction using this scale:

A Minor Pentatonic

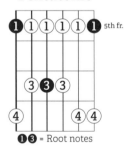

① ③ = Root notes

Playing Chords: Full Ami and Emi

Below are the full versions of the easy Ami and Emi chords you previously learned. Now compare the sound of the A and Ami, or the E and the Emi. They center on the same pitch, but sound different.

Ami

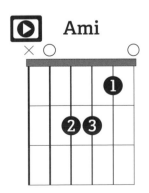

Emi

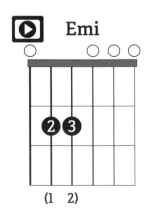

(1 2)

Play the following two progressions and pay attention to the difference in sound. You can select the strum pattern:

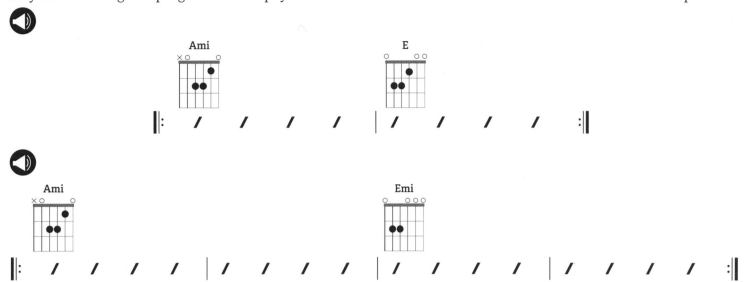

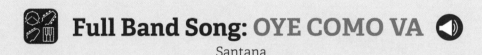

Santana

Form of Recording: Intro–Verse–Breakdown 1–Verse–Breakdown 1–Verse–Breakdown 1–Verse–Breakdown 2–Verse

Here is the main progression of the song:

Verse 🔊

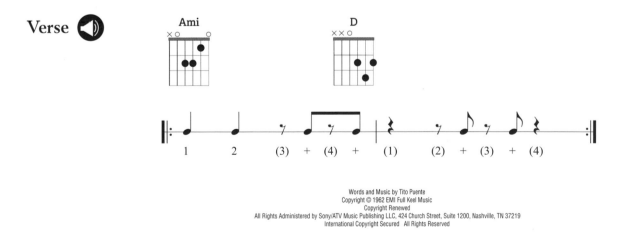

Here's the breakdown that happens periodically throughout the song. It happens first at the 30-second mark. On the Jam Track, the main riff is played four times through before the breakdown comes in.

Breakdown 1

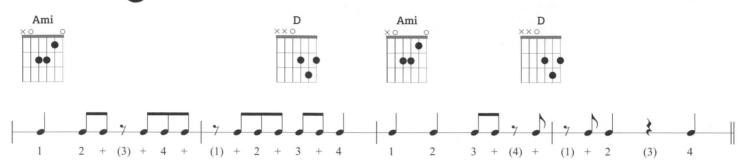

Here's one more section, which is played over an E chord. As before, the main riff alternates with this section on the Jam Track.

Breakdown 2

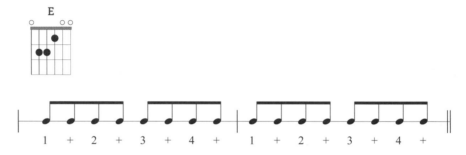

VERSE

Ami   **D**
Oye como va, mi ritmo.

Ami   **D**
Bueno pa gozar, mulata.

Ami   **D**
Oye como va, mi ritmo.

Ami   **D**
Bueno pa gozar, mulata.

SECTION 8

Instrument Technique: Riffs on 5th and 6th Strings

One way to keep your fingers nimble is to learn more riffs. Here are a few more that focus on strings 5 and 6.

COME AS YOU ARE 🔊
Nirvana

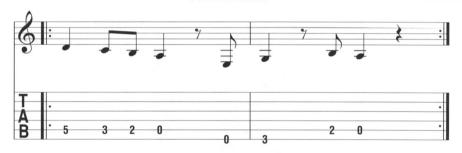

U CAN'T TOUCH THIS 🔊
MC Hammer

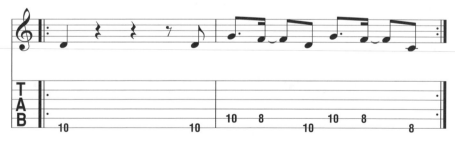

UPTOWN FUNK 🔊
Mark Ronson ft. Bruno Mars

Instrument Technique: The Bend ▶

To **bend** a note, play the fret shown in the tab and then pull the string down toward the floor or push up toward the ceiling. The pitch will go up as you bend. Bending to the exact pitch takes some practice, so play along with the Jam Track or the original recording to work on it.

THE MAN WHO SOLD THE WORLD 🔊
David Bowie

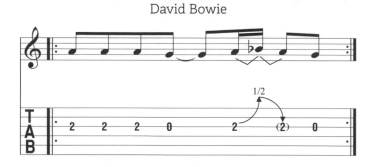

The fraction ("1/2") above the note means the bent note should sound one **half step** (or one fret) higher. So bending the 2nd fret one half step should sound like the 3rd fret on the same string.

In this next example, the "1/4" bend means to bend the string just a little bit. This will create a note that is "between the frets," which is more of an expressive effect than a specific pitch. Again, use the Jam Track or original recording as a guide and practice along with it to match the bend.

SUPERMASSIVE BLACK HOLE 🔊
Muse

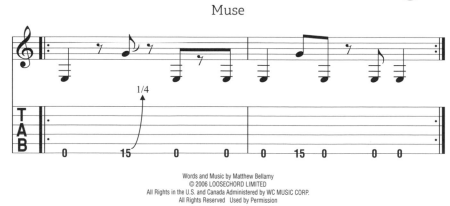

Instrument Technique: Syncopation and Muted Strums

Earlier, you played various syncopated strumming patterns. A common technique to add to these strumming patterns is the percussive muted string strum.

To get this sound, first lay the palm of your picking hand across all the strings near the bridge:

Then, without lifting your hand off the strings, strum through these muted strings. The strings should click, rather than ring out.

Muted strings are often notated with an "X." Mute the strings on beat 2 with this next song. Then, lift your palm off the strings before you play the upstroke on the "and" of beat 2. Practice this slowly until you can play the muted strum in one continuous motion. Try it out first with just the Emi chord:

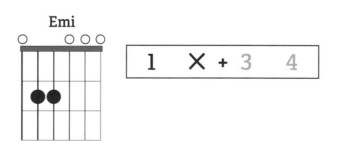

Now, try it with a song:

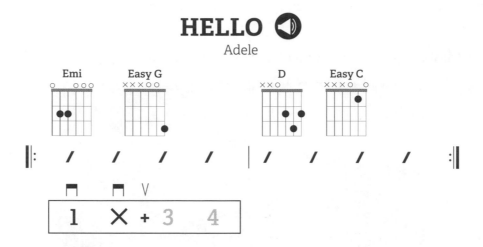

Use the same strumming pattern on this next song:

Try applying muted strumming to a song you played earlier using this syncopated reggae pattern:

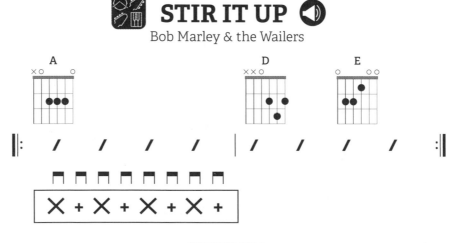

Full Band Song: WAKA WAKA
(THIS TIME FOR AFRICA)

Shakira

Form of Recording: Intro–Verse–Pre-Chorus–Chorus–Interlude–Verse–Pre-Chorus–Chorus–Bridge–Chorus

For this song, you will play the same chords for each section.

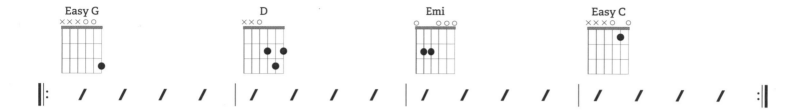

However, how you play those chords can vary from section to section. For the Verse, strum whole notes:

1   2   3   4

During the Chorus, you can emphasize the kick and snare drum pattern by plucking just the root notes of the chord before playing the full chord.

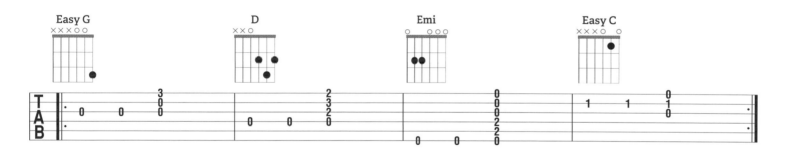

Words and Music by Shakira, Zolani Mahola, John Hill, Eugene Victor Doo Belley, Jean Ze Bella and Emile Kojidie
Copyright © 2010 Sony/ATV Music Publishing LLC, MyMPM Music, Freshly Ground, EMI April Music Inc., RodeoMan Music and Sony/ATV Music Publishing (Germany) Gmbh
All Rights Administered by Sony/ATV Music Publishing LLC, 424 Church Street, Suite 1200, Nashville, TN 37219
International Copyright Secured   All Rights Reserved

VERSE

G   D
You're a good soldier, choosing your battles.

      Emi   C
      Pick yourself up and dust yourself off and get back in the saddle.

G   D
You're on the front line, everyone's watching.

      Emi   C
      You know it's serious, we're getting closer, this isn't over.

G   D   Emi   C
The pressure's on, you feel it. But you got it all, believe it.

PRE-CHORUS

G   D
When you fall get up, oh, oh. And if you fall get up, eh, eh.

      Emi   C
      Tsamina mina zangalewa, 'cause this is Africa.

CHORUS

G   D   Emi   C
Tsamina mina, eh, eh. Waka waka, eh, eh. Tsamina mina zangalewa, this time for Africa.

VERSE

G   D   Emi
Listen to your God. This is our motto. Your time to shine,

                  C
      don't wait in line, y vamos por todo.

G   D   Emi
People are raising their expectations. Go on and feed them,

                  C
      this is your moment, no hesitation.

G   D   Emi   C
Today's your day, I feel it. You paved the way, believe it.

PRE-CHORUS

G   D
If you get down get up, oh, oh. When you get down get up, eh, eh.

      Emi   C
      Tsamina mina zangalewa, this time for Africa.

BRIDGE

G
Awabuye lamajoni, ipikipiki mama wa A to Z.

Bathi susa lamajoni, ipikipiki mama from East to West.

Bathi waka waka ma eh eh, waka waka ma eh eh,

Zonk' izizwe mazibuye, 'cause this is Africa.

Going Beyond: Sixteenth Notes

During the Pre-Chorus of "Waka Waka," try the guitar strumming pattern using **sixteenth notes**, which we haven't yet covered in this series. Use your ear to hear the snare drum hits on the recording, which are played in the same rhythm. Be sure to play these notes short by muting the strings right after you play them.

Music Theory: Transcribing Notation

Play through the melody of this song. The first four measures are written in tab. Then, write in the correct pitches on the traditional staff. The first note is provided for you.

LITTLE TALKS
Of Monsters and Men

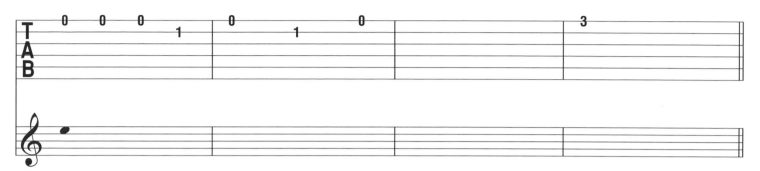

The last four measures are written below in staff notation. Write in the tab numbers. Don't worry about the rhythmic notation for now.

This last example has two new types of rhythmic symbols: the **dot** and the **tie**. When you see a dotted note, the dot adds half the value of the note to itself. So a **dotted quarter note** is one and a half beats.

Ties connect the notes. For example, the tied quarter and whole notes equal a total of five beats. You only pick the first note and then let it ring for five beats.

Playing Chords: Full C and G

Here is the full version of the easy C chord that you learned earlier. Practice it with the next song.

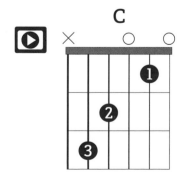

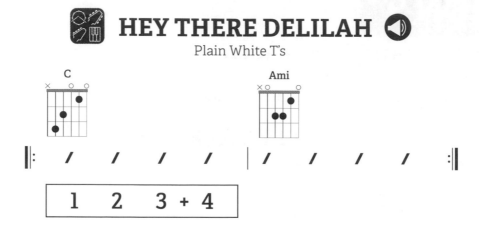

HEY THERE DELILAH

Plain White T's

Rather than lifting your first and second finger between these two chords, you can leave them on the strings and just move your third finger. The fingers that stay put are called **anchor fingers**.

Here is the full version of the easy G chord that you learned earlier. Try it out in the song that follows.

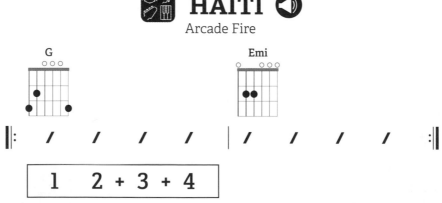

HAITI

Arcade Fire

This next song uses both G and C. Play G on beats 1 and 2, then switch to C and play it on the "and" of beat 3, and again on beat 4. In the second measure, play the same pattern but this time with the D and C chords.

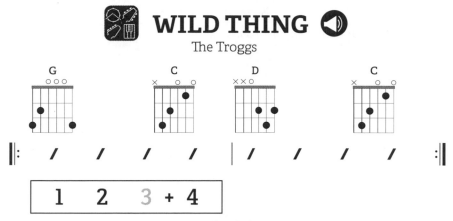

Below is one of the most popular chord progressions in all of popular music:

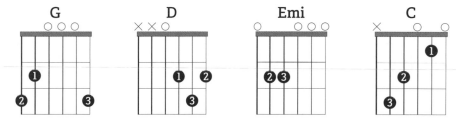

This progression can be found in many songs from the last 60 years, including "Where Is the Love," "Bored to Death," "Demons," "Apologize," "The Edge of Glory," "Someone Like You," and hundreds of others. Try it with the Chorus of the pop song "The Edge of Glory" by Lady Gaga.

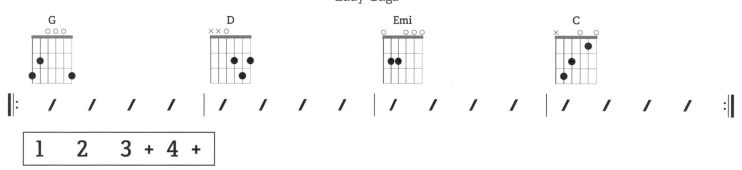

| G   D   Emi   C
I'm on the edge of glory, and I'm hanging on a moment of truth.

| G   D   Emi   C
Out on the edge of glory, and I'm hanging on a moment with you.

| G   D   Emi   C
I'm on the edge, the edge, the edge, the edge, the edge, the edge, the edge.

| G   D   Emi   C
I'm on the edge of glory, and I'm hanging on a moment with you.

| G
I'm on the edge with you.

Composition: Verse and Chorus ▶️

Now that you know more chords, you can use them to compose songs. Create a new four-chord verse and chorus, using any of the seven open chords you have already learned (A, Ami, C, D, E, Emi, and G). Try using a syncopated rhythm for either your verse or chorus.

Verse Chords:

‖: ／ ／ ／ ／ | ／ ／ ／ ／ | ／ ／ ／ ／ | ／ ／ ／ ／ :‖

Chorus Chords:

‖: ／ ／ ／ ／ | ／ ／ ／ ／ | ／ ／ ／ ／ | ／ ／ ／ ／ :‖

Improvisation: Major Pentatonic Scale 🔊 ▶️

The **major pentatonic scale** looks a lot like the minor pentatonic scale. The only difference between the two scales is which note feels like home, or the **tonic**. Here are a couple sample riffs you can play over the Jam Track.

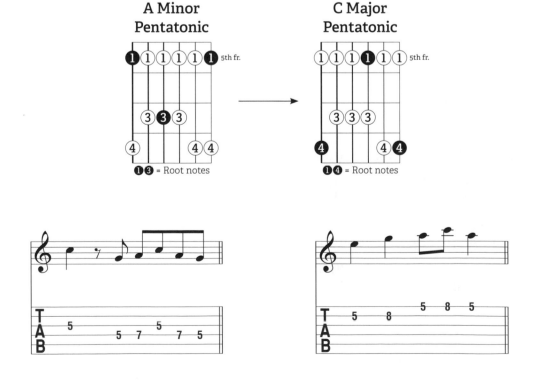

A Minor Pentatonic   **C Major Pentatonic**

❶❸ = Root notes   ❶❹ = Root notes

42

Try the scale over a few familiar progressions.

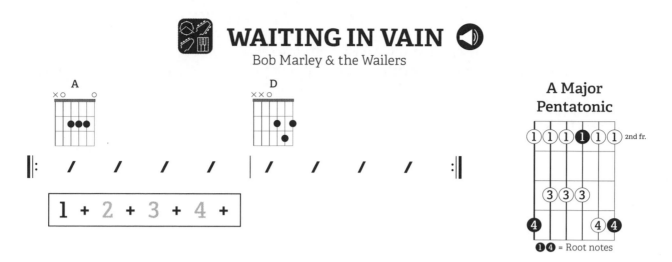

WAITING IN VAIN
Bob Marley & the Wailers

The scale pattern for this next song uses open strings and different fingerings than the previous pattern, but it has the same shape.

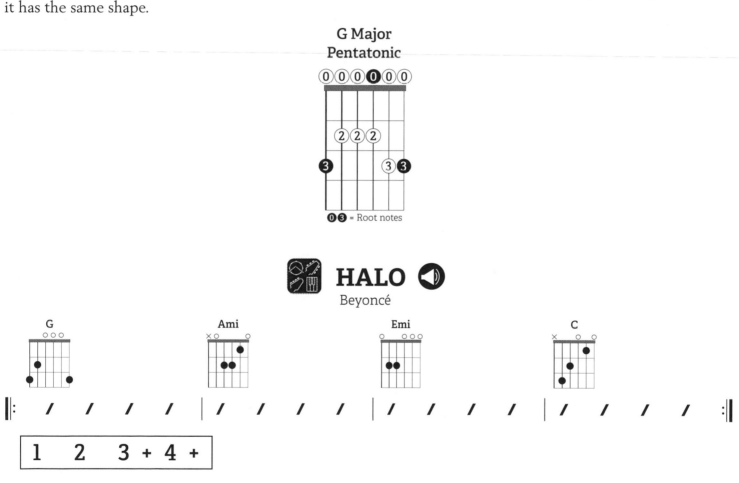

HALO
Beyoncé

Full Band Song: BEST DAY OF MY LIFE

American Authors

Form of Recording: Intro–Verse–Pre-Chorus–Chorus–Verse–Pre-Chorus–Chorus–Bridge–Chorus

This song combines several of the skills you have learned so far: chords, bends, riffs, and a solo. In the fourth bar of the Pre-Chorus, there is a measure with no chord. Don't play during that measure of music.

Verse/Chorus

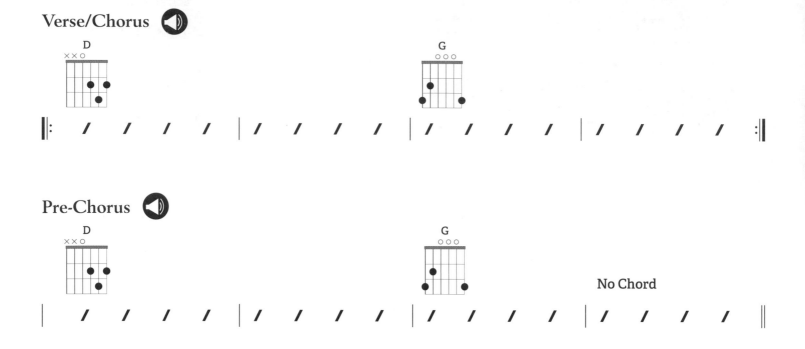

Pre-Chorus

Bridge

Chorus Riff

This song doesn't have a guitar solo, but you can add one to your performance of the song. Use the D major pentatonic scale because the song is in the **key** of D major.

D Major Pentatonic

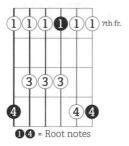

● ❹ = Root notes

VERSE

D
I had a dream so big and loud. I jumped so high I touched the clouds.

G
Whoa-o-o-o-o-oh. Whoa-o-o-o-o-oh.

D
I stretched my hands out to the sky. We danced with monsters through the night.

G
Whoa-o-o-o-o-oh. Whoa-o-o-o-o-oh.

PRE-CHORUS

D   Emi
I'm never gonna look back, whoa. I'm never gonna give it up, no. Please don't wake me now.

CHORUS

D   G
Wo-o-o-o-oo! This is gonna be the best day of my life, my life.

D   G
Wo-o-o-o-oo! This is gonna be the best day of my life, my life.

VERSE

D
I howled at the moon with friends. And then the sun came crashing in.

G
Whoa-o-o-o-o-oh. Whoa-o-o-o-o-oh.

         D
But all the possibilities, no limits just epiphanies.

G
Whoa-o-o-o-o-oh. Whoa-o-o-o-o-oh.

BRIDGE

D
I hear it calling outside my window.

I feel it in my soul, soul.

The stars were burning so bright,

The sun was out 'til midnight.

I say we lose control, control.

SECTION 10

Instrument Technique: Pentatonic Riffs

Here are a few more pentatonic riffs so you can see the scale in action.

LOVE ON THE WEEKEND
John Mayer

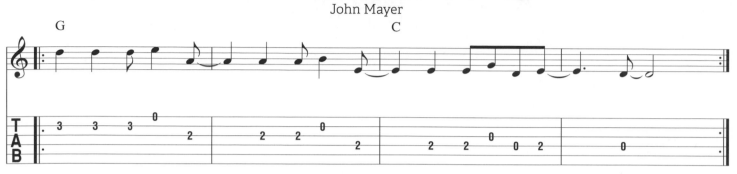

This next riff is played with a **shuffle feel**. This means the eighth notes are played in an uneven rhythm. You've probably heard this popular sound before in countless blues, rock, pop, and jazz songs. Listen to the original recording of this classic blues riff and play with the Jam Track to get a feel for it.

MANNISH BOY
Muddy Waters

Music Theory: Tab vs. Notation

Check out the pentatonic riff from the song below. In the first example, try playing it using just staff notation.

CLOSER
The Chainsmokers ft. Halsey

One of the difficulties with guitar and notation is that you can play the same notes in multiple places on the fretboard. Here are two ways to play it, this time shown with tab.

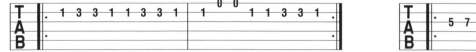
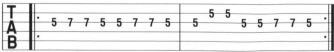

The sound quality will change depending on where you choose to play this melody. You can try different ways and listen for which you like best.

Instrument Technique: Chord Variations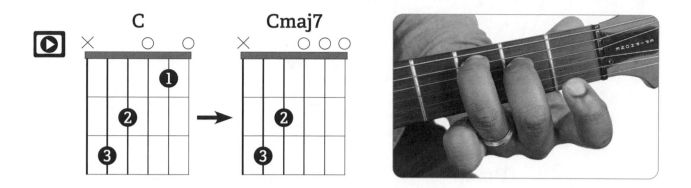

You can create new chords by adding or removing fingers to add color to chords you already know.

By lifting the first finger from the C chord, you change C to Cmaj7 ("C major seven"):

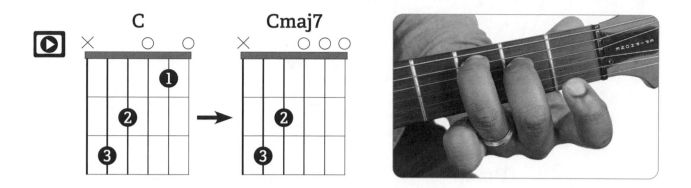

Ami becomes an Ami7 ("A minor seven") when you remove your third finger.

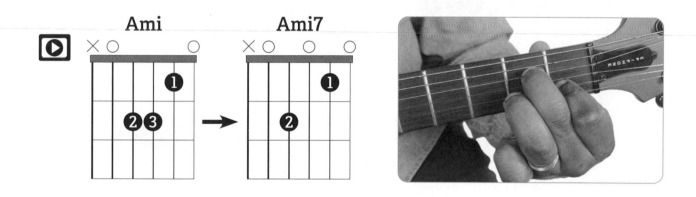

Try switching between them using this song's chord progression:

BULLETPROOF... I WISH I WAS
Radiohead

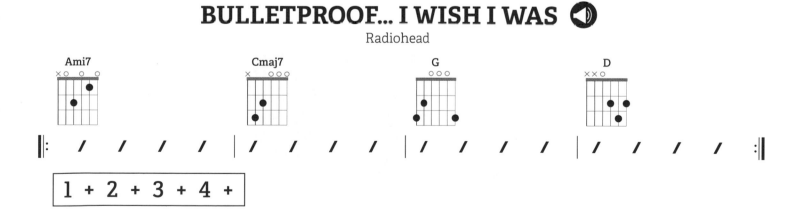

These are just a couple examples of chords you can create with small alterations. Spend some time removing and adding fingers to the chords you already know to make different sounds. Here are a few more examples using the D chord:

D

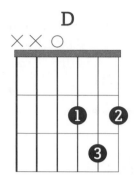

Dmaj7

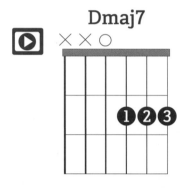

Dsus2

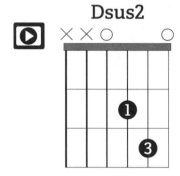

Dsus4

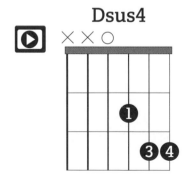

Using this trick, you can also play chords that you haven't learned yet, such as the F chord. Instead, play Fmaj7:

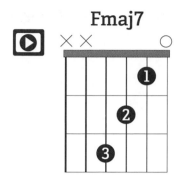

Several of these chords will be used in the next Full Band Song.

Playing Chords: Dmi

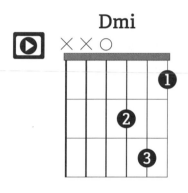

Here is a song that uses Dmi:

UPTOWN FUNK
Mark Ronson ft. Bruno Mars

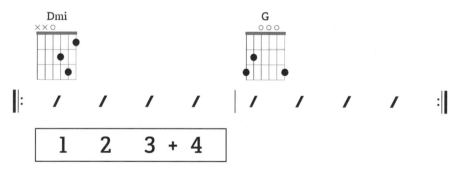

Full Band Song: KICK, PUSH

Lupe Fiasco

Form of Recording: Verse–Chorus–Verse–Chorus–Verse–Chorus

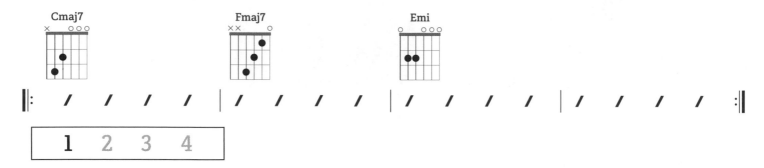

Verse/Chorus Riff

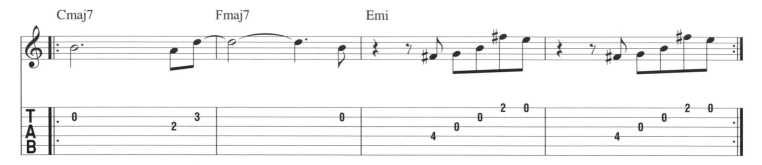

VERSE

First got it when he was six, didn't know any tricks. Matter fact,

First time he got on it he slipped, landed on his hip and bust his lip.

For a week he had to talk with a lisp, like this.

Now we can end the story right here,

But shorty didn't quit, it was something in the air, yea.

He said it was somethin' so appealing. He couldn't fight the feelin'.

Somethin' about it, he knew he couldn't doubt it, couldn't understand it,

Brand it, since the first kickflip he landed, uh. Labeled a misfit, abandoned,

Ca-kunk, ca-kunk, kunk. His neighbors couldn't stand it, so he was banished to the park.

Started in the morning, wouldn't stop till after dark, yea.

When they said "it's getting late in here, so I'm sorry young man, there's no skating here."

CHORUS

So we kick, push, kick, push, kick, push, kick, push, coast.

And the way he roll just a rebel to the world with no place to go.

So we kick, push, kick, push, kick, push, kick, push, coast.

So come and skate with me, just a rebel looking for a place to be.

So let's kick, and push, and coast.

VERSE

Uh, uh, uh. My man got a lil' older, became a better roller (yea).

No helmet, hell-bent on killin' himself, was what his momma said.

But he was feelin' himself, got a lil' more swagger in his style.

Met his girlfriend, she was clappin' in the crowd.

Love is what was happening to him now, uh. He said "I would marry you but I'm engaged to

These aerials and varials, and I don't think this board is strong enough to carry two."

She said "beau, I weigh 120 pounds. Now, lemme make one thing clear, I don't need to ride

yours, I got mine right here." So she took him to a spot he didn't know about,

Somewhere in the apartment parking lot, she said, "I don't normally take dates in here."

Security came and said, "I'm sorry there's no skating here."

CHORUS

So they kick, push, kick, push, kick, push, kick, push, coast.

And the way they roll, just lovers intertwined with no place to go.

And so they kick, push, kick, push, kick, push, kick, push, coast.

So come and skate with me, just a rebel looking for a place to be.

So let's kick, and push, and coast.

VERSE

Yea uh, yea, yea. Before he knew he had a crew that wasn't no punk

In they Spitfire shirts and SB Dunks. They would push, till they couldn't skate no more.

Office buildings, lobbies wasn't safe no more.

And it wasn't like they wasn't getting chased no more,

Just the freedom is better than breathing, they said.

An escape route, they used to escape out when things got crazy they needed to break out.

(They'd head) to any place with stairs, and good grinds the world was theirs, uh.

And they four wheels would take them there,

Until the cops came and said, "There's no skating here."

CHORUS

So they kick, push, kick, push, kick, push, kick, push, coast.

And the way they roll, just rebels without a cause with no place to go.

And so they kick, push, kick, push, kick, push, kick, push, coast.

So come roll with me, just a rebel looking for a place to be.

So let's kick, and push, and coast.

SECTION 11

Music Theory: Blues Scale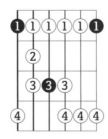

BAD

Michael Jackson

SUNSHINE OF YOUR LOVE

Cream

Both of these riffs use the **blues scale**. You can use this scale to write riffs or play solos. The blues scale is similar to the minor pentatonic scale with an added "blue" note. There is no fret reference number shown here because this scale shape can be moved up and down the neck of the guitar, just like the pentatonic scales.

Try writing a riff using notes in the blues scale:

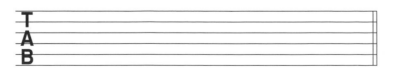

Instrument Technique: Slides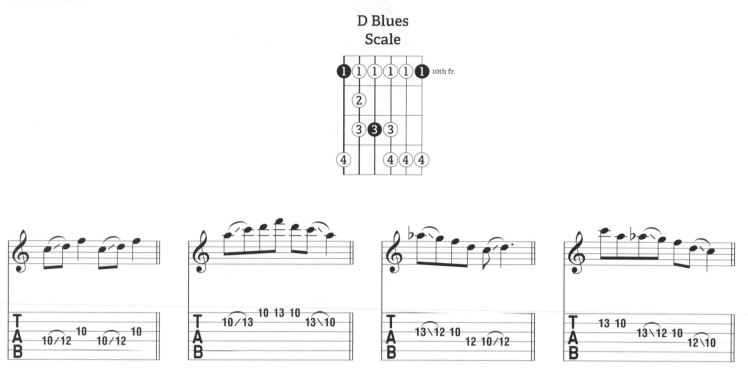

There are several different types of **slides** you can play on the guitar. We will focus on a common slide that moves from one note to another on the same string without lifting off the fretboard. Similar to hammer-ons and pull-offs, the slur in the notation tells you not to pick the second note. Try these examples using the D blues scale:

Play a solo over the next song using the D blues scale and add some slides to it, along with hammer-ons and pull-offs. If you find something cool, write in the tab below!

EVIL WAYS

Santana

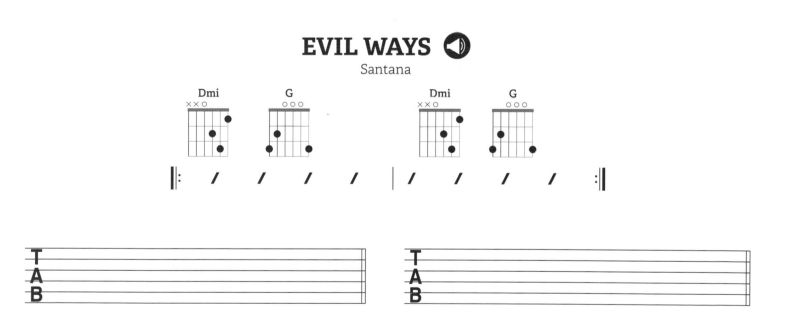

Instrument Technique: Power Chords

Power chords will allow you to play even more songs. Every power chord has the same shape that can be moved up or down the guitar. Start with a two-note power chord, A5:

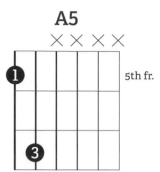

You can also play a power chord with three fingers. Try them with the next song.

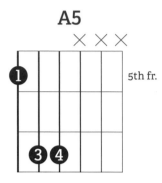

STRAY CAT STRUT
Stray Cats

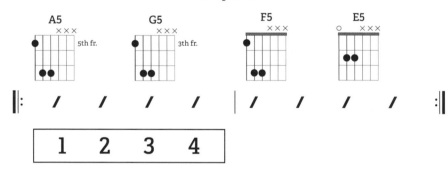

Power chords can be played on the 5th string as well:

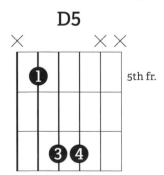

You can also finger the three-note power chords using a **barre**, in which you fret two notes with one finger. In this case, you can use your ring or pinky finger to lay flat across the two higher notes in the chord, holding them both down with one finger.

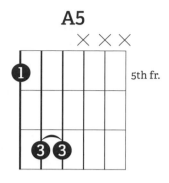

A5

5th fr.

Here is a song that uses power chords on both the 6th and 5th strings:

SMELLS LIKE TEEN SPIRIT

Nirvana

F5   Bb5   Ab5   Db5

4th fr.   4th fr.

Composition: Composing with Power Chords

To write a song with power chords, pick a string number (5 or 6) and a fret number (1–10). Play a power chord at that location with your first finger on that fret and string. Pick four chords this way and write a rhythm to play them with.

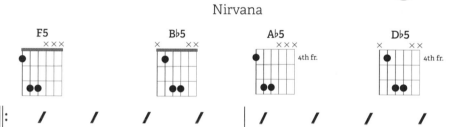

Full Band Song: UMBRELLA

Rihanna

Form of Recording: Intro–Verse–Chorus–Verse–Chorus–Bridge–Chorus

For this song, you can play this riff in the Intro and first Verse:

Intro/Verse

Here are the chords for the Verse:

Verse

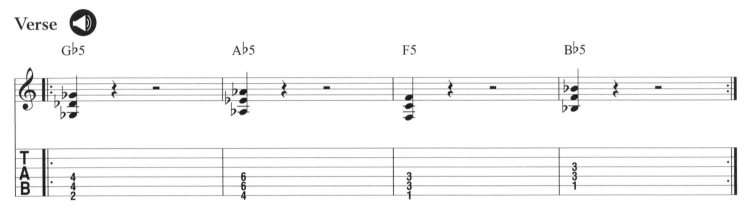

In the Chorus section, you can play sustained power chords:

Chorus

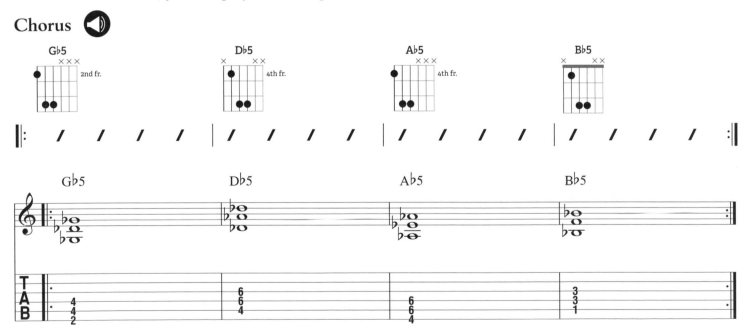

Often in music, material is repeated but with different endings. To show this, we can write **first and second endings** in the notation. These are the measures under the brackets labeled "1." and "2." To play this, perform the first four measures of Verse 2 below and then repeat. When playing it the second time, skip the first ending and play the second ending.

Verse 2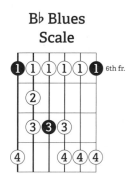

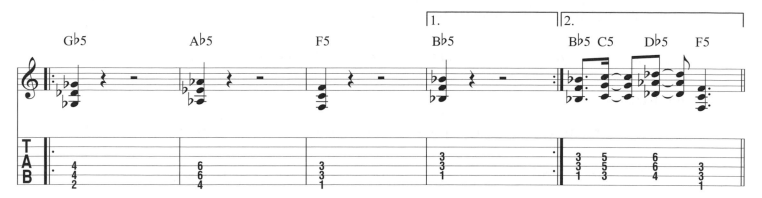

You can also play power chords in the Bridge, which has a first and second ending as well. Play the four measures before the repeat sign the first time, then skip the first ending the second time and jump to the second ending.

Bridge

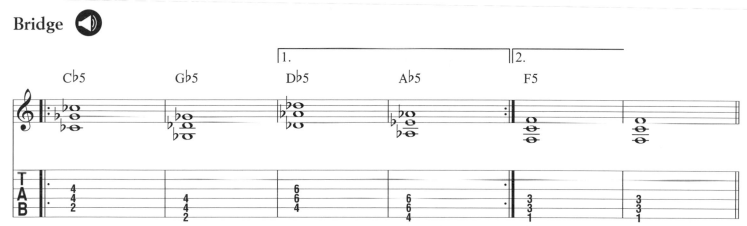

You can use the B♭ blues scale to solo over all the sections except the Bridge.

**B♭ Blues
Scale**

57

VERSE

G♭5   **A♭5**
You have my heart, and we'll never be worlds apart.

          F5   **B♭5**
Maybe in magazines, but you'll still be my star.

          G♭5   **A♭5**
Baby, 'cause in the dark you can't see shiny cars.

                    F5   **B♭5**
And that's when you need me there, with you I'll always share, because...

CHORUS

G♭5   **D♭5**   **A♭5**
When the sun shines, we'll shine together. Told you I'd be here forever.

                    B♭5
Said I'll always be your friend. Took an oath, I'mma stick it out 'til the end.

G♭5   **D♭5**   **A♭5**
Now that it's raining more than ever, know that we'll still have each other.

                    B♭5   **G♭5**
You can stand under my umbrella. You can stand under my umbrella.

          D♭5   **A♭5**
(Ella, ella, eh, eh, eh.) Under my umbrella.

          B♭5   **G♭5**
(Ella, ella, eh, eh, eh.) Under my umbrella.

          D♭5   **A♭5**
(Ella, ella, eh, eh, eh.) Under my umbrella.

          B♭5
(Ella, ella, eh, eh, eh, eh, eh, eh.)

VERSE

          G♭5   **A♭5**
These fancy things, will never come in between.

                    F5   **B♭5**
You're part of my entity, here for infinity.

                    G♭5   **A♭5**
When the war has took its part, when the world has dealt its cards,

          F5   **B♭5**
If the hand is hard, together we'll mend your heart.

BRIDGE

C♭5   **G♭5**
You can run into my arms. It's OK, don't be alarmed.

          D♭5   **A♭5**
Come here to me. There's no distance in between our love.

C♭5   **G♭5**
So go on and let the rain pour.

                              F5
I'll be all you need and more, because...

Full Band Song: ZOMBIE

The Cranberries

Form of Recording: Intro–Verse–Chorus–Verse–Chorus–Bridge–Chorus–Outro

This last song combines several of the elements you've learned in this book:

- Open chords
- Power chords
- Chord variations
- Tab reading
- Hammer-ons
- Pull-offs

Here is the whole song. Choose your own strum patterns for the different sections. For the Chorus, you can use the tab part for the power chords.

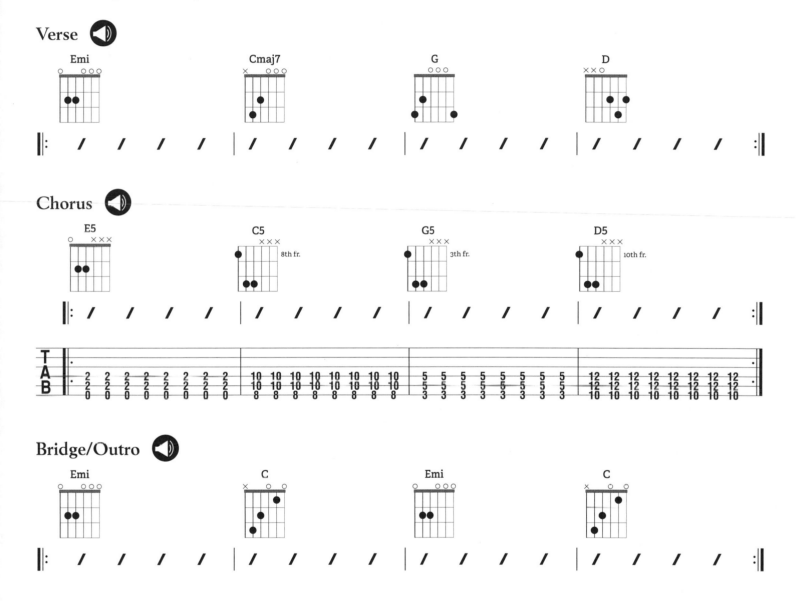

Bridge/Outro

Here is the guitar riff at the end of the Chorus:

Here is the guitar riff played during the Outro:

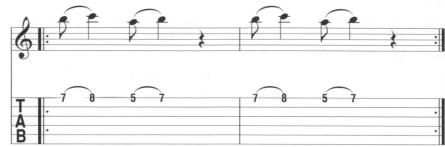

VERSE
Emi   Cmaj7   G   D
Another head hangs lowly, child is slowly taken.

Emi   Cmaj7   G   D
And the violence caused such silence. Who are we mistaken?

        Emi   Cmaj7   G   D
But you see it's not me, it's not my family. In your head, in your head they are fighting,

        Emi   Cmaj7
With their tanks, and their bombs, and their bombs, and their guns.

       G   D
In your head, in your head they are crying.

CHORUS
      E5   C5   G5   D5
In your head, in your head, zombie, zombie, zombie, hey, hey.

         E5   C5   G5   D5
What's in your head, in your head, zombie, zombie, zombie, hey, hey, hey?

VERSE
Emi   Cmaj7   G   D
Another mother's breakin' heart is taking over.

Emi   Cmaj7   G   D
When the violence causes silence, we must be mistaken.

        Emi   Cmaj7   G   D
It's the same old theme since nineteen-sixteen. In your head, in your head they're still fighting,

        Emi   Cmaj7
With their tanks, and their bombs, and their bombs, and their guns.

       G   D
In your head, in your head they are dying.

CHORUS
      E5   C5   G5   D5
In your head, in your head, zombie, zombie, zombie, hey, hey.

         E5   C5   G5   D5
What's in your head, in your head, zombie, zombie, zombie. Hey, hey, hey?

GUITAR PLAY-ALONG

INCLUDES TAB   AUDIO ACCESS INCLUDED

This series will help you play your favorite songs quickly and easily. Just follow the tab and listen to the audio to hear how the guitar should sound, and then play along using the separate backing tracks.

Playback tools are provided for slowing down the tempo without changing pitch and looping challenging parts. The melody and lyrics are included in the book so that you can sing or simply follow along.

1. ROCK
00699570....................$17.99

2. ACOUSTIC
00699569....................$17.99

3. HARD ROCK
00699573....................$19.99

4. POP/ROCK
00699571....................$16.99

5. THREE CHORD SONGS
00300985....................$16.99

6. '90S ROCK
00298615....................$16.99

7. BLUES
00699575....................$19.99

8. ROCK
00699585....................$16.99

9. EASY ACOUSTIC SONGS
00151708....................$16.99

11. EARLY ROCK
00699579....................$17.99

12. ROCK POP
00291724....................$17.99

14. BLUES ROCK
00699582....................$17.99

15. R&B
00699583....................$17.99

16. JAZZ
00699584....................$17.99

17. COUNTRY
00699588....................$17.99

18. ACOUSTIC ROCK
00699577....................$15.95

20. ROCKABILLY
00699580....................$17.99

21. SANTANA
00174525....................$19.99

22. CHRISTMAS
00699600....................$15.99

23. SURF
00699635....................$17.99

24. ERIC CLAPTON
00699649....................$19.99

25. THE BEATLES
00198265....................$19.99

26. ELVIS PRESLEY
00699643....................$17.99

27. DAVID LEE ROTH
00699645....................$16.95

29. BOB SEGER
00699647....................$16.99

30. KISS
00699644....................$17.99

32. THE OFFSPRING
00699653....................$14.95

33. ACOUSTIC CLASSICS
00699656....................$19.99

35. HAIR METAL
00699660....................$19.99

36. SOUTHERN ROCK
00699661....................$19.99

37. ACOUSTIC UNPLUGGED
00699662....................$22.99

39. '80S METAL
00699664....................$17.99

40. INCUBUS
00699668....................$17.95

41. ERIC CLAPTON
00699669....................$17.99

42. COVER BAND HITS
00211597....................$16.99

43. LYNYRD SKYNYRD
00699681....................$22.99

44. JAZZ GREATS
00699689....................$19.99

45. TV THEMES
00699718....................$14.95

46. MAINSTREAM ROCK
00699722....................$16.95

47. HENDRIX SMASH HITS
00699723....................$22.99

48. AEROSMITH CLASSICS
00699724....................$19.99

49. STEVIE RAY VAUGHAN
00699725....................$19.99

50. VAN HALEN 1978-1984
00110269....................$19.99

51. ALTERNATIVE '90S
00699727....................$14.99

52. FUNK
00699728....................$17.99

53. DISCO
00699729....................$14.99

55. POP METAL
00699731....................$14.95

57. GUNS N' ROSES
00159922....................$19.99

59. CHET ATKINS
00702347....................$22.99

60. 3 DOORS DOWN
00699774....................$14.95

62. CHRISTMAS CAROLS
00699798....................$12.95

63. CREEDENCE CLEARWATER REVIVAL
00699802....................$17.99

64. OZZY OSBOURNE
00699803....................$22.99

66. THE ROLLING STONES
00699807....................$19.99

67. BLACK SABBATH
00699808....................$17.99

68. PINK FLOYD – DARK SIDE OF THE MOON
00699809....................$17.99

71. CHRISTIAN ROCK
00699824....................$14.95

74. SIMPLE STRUMMING SONGS
00151706....................$19.99

75. TOM PETTY
00699882....................$19.99

76. COUNTRY HITS
00699884....................$16.99

77. BLUEGRASS
00699910....................$17.99

78. NIRVANA
00700132....................$17.99

79. NEIL YOUNG
00700133....................$24.99

81. ROCK ANTHOLOGY
00700176....................$24.99

82. EASY ROCK SONGS
00700177....................$17.99

84. STEELY DAN
00700200....................$19.99

85. THE POLICE
00700269....................$17.99

86. BOSTON
00700465....................$19.99

87. ACOUSTIC WOMEN
00700763....................$14.99

88. GRUNGE
00700467....................$16.99

89. REGGAE
00700468....................$15.99

90. CLASSICAL POP
00700469....................$14.99

91. BLUES INSTRUMENTALS
00700505....................$19.99

92. EARLY ROCK INSTRUMENTALS
00700506....................$17.99

93. ROCK INSTRUMENTALS
00700507....................$17.99

94. SLOW BLUES
00700508....................$16.99

95. BLUES CLASSICS
00700509....................$17.99

96. BEST COUNTRY HITS
00211615....................$16.99

97. CHRISTMAS CLASSICS
00236542....................$14.99

99. ZZ TOP
00700762....................$17.99

100. B.B. KING
00700466....................$17.99

101. SONGS FOR BEGINNERS
00701917....................$14.99

102. CLASSIC PUNK
00700769....................$14.99

104. DUANE ALLMAN
00700846....................$22.99

105. LATIN
00700939....................$16.99

106. WEEZER
00700958....................$17.99

107. CREAM
00701069....................$17.99

108. THE WHO
00701053........................$17.99

109. STEVE MILLER
00701054........................$19.99

110. SLIDE GUITAR HITS
00701055........................$17.99

111. JOHN MELLENCAMP
00701056........................$14.99

112. QUEEN
00701052........................$16.99

113. JIM CROCE
00701058........................$19.99

114. BON JOVI
00701060........................$17.99

115. JOHNNY CASH
00701070........................$17.99

116. THE VENTURES
00701124........................$17.99

117. BRAD PAISLEY
00701224........................$16.99

118. ERIC JOHNSON
00701353........................$19.99

119. AC/DC CLASSICS
00701356........................$19.99

120. PROGRESSIVE ROCK
00701457........................$14.99

121. U2
00701508........................$17.99

122. CROSBY, STILLS & NASH
00701610........................$16.99

123. LENNON & McCARTNEY ACOUSTIC
00701614........................$16.99

124. SMOOTH JAZZ
00200664........................$17.99

125. JEFF BECK
00701687........................$19.99

126. BOB MARLEY
00701701........................$19.99

127. 1970S ROCK
00701739........................$17.99

129. MEGADETH
00701741........................$17.99

130. IRON MAIDEN
00701742........................$19.99

131. 1990S ROCK
00701743........................$14.99

132. COUNTRY ROCK
00701757........................$15.99

135. MINOR BLUES
00151350........................$17.99

136. GUITAR THEMES
00701922........................$14.99

137. IRISH TUNES
00701966........................$17.99

138. BLUEGRASS CLASSICS
00701967........................$17.99

139. GARY MOORE
00702370........................$19.99

140. MORE STEVIE RAY VAUGHAN
00702396........................$24.99

141. ACOUSTIC HITS
00702401........................$16.99

142. GEORGE HARRISON
00237697........................$17.99

143. SLASH
00702425........................$19.99

144. DJANGO REINHARDT
00702531........................$17.99

145. DEF LEPPARD
00702532........................$19.99

146. ROBERT JOHNSON
00702533........................$16.99

147. SIMON & GARFUNKEL
14041591........................$19.99

148. BOB DYLAN
14041592........................$19.99

149. AC/DC HITS
14041593........................$19.99

150. ZAKK WYLDE
02501717........................$19.99

151. J.S. BACH
02501730........................$16.99

152. JOE BONAMASSA
02501751........................$24.99

153. RED HOT CHILI PEPPERS
00702990........................$22.99

155. ERIC CLAPTON – FROM THE ALBUM UNPLUGGED
00703085........................$19.99

156. SLAYER
00703770........................$19.99

157. FLEETWOOD MAC
00101382........................$17.99

159. WES MONTGOMERY
00102593........................$22.99

160. T-BONE WALKER
00102641........................$17.99

161. THE EAGLES – ACOUSTIC
00102659........................$19.99

162. THE EAGLES HITS
00102667........................$19.99

163. PANTERA
00103036........................$19.99

164. VAN HALEN 1986-1995
00110270........................$19.99

165. GREEN DAY
00210343........................$17.99

166. MODERN BLUES
00700764........................$16.99

167. DREAM THEATER
00111938........................$24.99

168. KISS
00113421........................$17.99

170. THREE DAYS GRACE
00117337........................$16.99

171. JAMES BROWN
00117420........................$16.99

172. THE DOOBIE BROTHERS
00119670........................$17.99

173. TRANS-SIBERIAN ORCHESTRA
00119907........................$19.99

174. SCORPIONS
00122119........................$19.99

175. MICHAEL SCHENKER
00122127........................$19.99

176. BLUES BREAKERS WITH JOHN MAYALL & ERIC CLAPTON
00122132........................$19.99

177. ALBERT KING
00123271........................$17.99

178. JASON MRAZ
00124165........................$17.99

179. RAMONES
00127073........................$17.99

180. BRUNO MARS
00129706........................$16.99

181. JACK JOHNSON
00129854........................$16.99

182. SOUNDGARDEN
00138161........................$17.99

183. BUDDY GUY
00138240........................$17.99

184. KENNY WAYNE SHEPHERD
00138258........................$17.99

185. JOE SATRIANI
00139457........................$19.99

186. GRATEFUL DEAD
00139459........................$17.99

187. JOHN DENVER
00140839........................$19.99

188. MÖTLEY CRUE
00141145........................$19.99

189. JOHN MAYER
00144350........................$22.99

190. DEEP PURPLE
00146152........................$19.99

191. PINK FLOYD CLASSICS
00146164........................$17.99

192. JUDAS PRIEST
00151352........................$19.99

193. STEVE VAI
00156028........................$19.99

195. METALLICA: 1983-1988
00234291........................$24.99

196. METALLICA: 1991-2016
00234292........................$22.99

HAL•LEONARD®

For complete songlists, visit
Hal Leonard online at
www.halleonard.com

Prices, contents, and availability subject to
change without notice.

FIRST 50

Books in the First 50 series contain easy to intermediate arrangements for must-know songs.
Each arrangement is simple and streamlined, yet still captures the essence of the tune.

First 50 Baroque Pieces
You Should Play on Guitar
Includes selections by Johann Sebastian Bach, Robert de Visée, Ernst Gottlieb Baron, Santiago de Murcia, Antonio Vivaldi, Sylvius Leopold Weiss, and more.
00322567...$14.99

First 50 Bluegrass Solos
You Should Play on Guitar
I Am a Man of Constant Sorrow • Long Journey Home • Molly and Tenbrooks • Old Joe Clark • Rocky Top • Salty Dog Blues • and more.
00298574...$16.99

First 50 Blues Songs
You Should Play on Guitar
All Your Love (I Miss Loving) • Bad to the Bone • Born Under a Bad Sign • Dust My Broom • Hoodoo Man Blues • Little Red Rooster • Love Struck Baby • Pride and Joy • Smoking Gun • Still Got the Blues • The Thrill Is Gone • You Shook Me • and more.
00235790...$17.99

First 50 Blues Turnarounds
You Should Play on Guitar
You'll learn cool turnarounds in the styles of these jazz legends: John Lee Hooker, Robert Johnson, Joe Pass, Jimmy Rogers, Hubert Sumlin, Stevie Ray Vaughan, T-Bone Walker, Muddy Waters, and more.
00277469...$14.99

First 50 Chords
You Should Play on Guitar
American Pie • Back in Black • Brown Eyed Girl • Landslide • Let It Be • Riptide • Summer of '69 • Take Me Home, Country Roads • Won't Get Fooled Again • You've Got a Friend • and more.
00300255 Guitar...................................$12.99

First 50 Classical Pieces
You Should Play on Guitar
Includes compositions by J.S. Bach, Augustin Rarrios, Matteo Carcassi, Domenico Scarlatti, Fernando Sor, Francisco Tárrega, Robert de Visée, Antonio Vivaldi and many more.
00155414...$16.99

First 50 Folk Songs
You Should Play on Guitar
Amazing Grace • Down by the Riverside • Home on the Range • I've Been Working on the Railroad • Kumbaya • Man of Constant Sorrow • Oh! Susanna • This Little Light of Mine • When the Saints Go Marching In • The Yellow Rose of Texas • and more.
00235868...$16.99

First 50 Guitar Duets
You Should Play
Chopsticks • Clocks • Eleanor Rigby • Game of Thrones Theme • Hallelujah • Linus and Lucy (from *A Charlie Brown Christmas*) • Memory (from *Cats*) • Over the Rainbow (from *The Wizard of Oz*) • Star Wars (Main Theme) • What a Wonderful World • You Raise Me Up • and more.
00319706...$14.99

First 50 Jazz Standards
You Should Play on Guitar
All the Things You Are • Body and Soul • Don't Get Around Much Anymore • Fly Me to the Moon (In Other Words) • The Girl from Ipanema (Garota De Ipanema) • I Got Rhythm • Laura • Misty • Night and Day • Satin Summertime • When I Fall in Love • and more.
00198594 Solo Guitar.......................$16.99

First 50 Kids' Songs
You Should Play on Guitar
Do-Re-Mi • Hakuna Matata • Let It Go • My Favorite Things • Puff the Magic Dragon • Take Me Out to the Ball Game • Won't You Be My Neighbor? (It's a Beautiful Day in the Neighborhood) • and more.
00300500...$17.99

First 50 Licks
You Should Play on Guitar
Licks presented include the styles of legendary guitarists like Eric Clapton, Buddy Guy, Jimi Hendrix, B.B. King, Randy Rhoads, Carlos Santana, Stevie Ray Vaughan and many more.
00278875 Book/Online Audio..........$14.99

First 50 Riffs
You Should Play on Guitar
All Right Now • Back in Black • Barracuda • Carry on Wayward Son • Crazy Train • La Grange • Layla • Seven Nation Army • Smoke on the Water • Sunday Bloody Sunday • Sunshine of Your Love • Sweet Home Alabama • Working Man • and more.
00277366...$17.99

First 50 Rock Songs You Should
Play on Electric Guitar
All Along the Watchtower • Beat It • Brown Eyed Girl • Cocaine • Detroit Rock City • Hallelujah • (I Can't Get No) Satisfaction • Oh, Pretty Woman • Pride and Joy • Seven Nation Army • Should I Stay or Should I Go • Smells like Teen Spirit • Smoke on the Water • When I Come Around • You Really Got Me • and more.
00131159...$16.99

First 50 Songs by the Beatles You
Should Play on Guitar
All You Need Is Love • Blackbird • Come Together • Eleanor Rigby • Hey Jude • I Want to Hold Your Hand • Let It Be • Ob-La-Di, Ob-La-Da • She Loves You • Twist and Shout • Yellow Submarine • Yesterday • and more.
00295323...$24.99

First 50 Songs
You Should Fingerpick on Guitar
Annie's Song • Blackbird • The Boxer • Classical Gas • Dust in the Wind • Fire and Rain • Greensleeves • Road Trippin' • Shape of My Heart • Tears in Heaven • Time in a Bottle • Vincent (Starry Starry Night) • and more.
00149269...$16.99

First 50 Songs You Should
Play on 12-String Guitar
California Dreamin' • Closer to the Heart • Free Fallin' • Give a Little Bit • Hotel California • Leaving on a Jet Plane • Life by the Drop • Over the Hills and Far Away • Solsbury Hill • Space Oddity • Wish You Were Here • You Wear It Well • and more.
00287559...$19.99

First 50 Songs You Should Play on
Acoustic Guitar
Against the Wind • Boulevard of Broken Dreams • Champagne Supernova • Every Rose Has Its Thorn • Fast Car • Free Fallin' • Layla • Let Her Go • Mean • One • Ring of Fire • Signs • Stairway to Heaven • Trouble • Wagon Wheel • Yellow • Yesterday • and more.
00131209...$16.99

First 50 Songs
You Should Play on Bass
Blister in the Sun • I Got You (I Feel Good) • Livin' on a Prayer • Low Rider • Money • Monkey Wrench • My Generation • Roxanne • Should I Stay or Should I Go • Uptown Funk • What's Going On • With or Without You • Yellow • and more.
00149189...$16.99

First 50 Songs
You Should Play on Solo Guitar
Africa • All of Me • Blue Skies • California Dreamin' • Change the World • Crazy • Dream a Little Dream of Me • Every Breath You Take • Hallelujah • Wonderful Tonight • Yesterday • You Raise Me Up • Your Song • and more.
00288843...$19.99

First 50 Songs
You Should Strum on Guitar
American Pie • Blowin' in the Wind • Daughter • Hey, Soul Sister • Home • I Will Wait • Losing My Religion • Mrs. Robinson • No Woman No Cry • Peaceful Easy Feeling • Rocky Mountain High • Sweet Caroline • Teardrops on My Guitar • Wonderful Tonight • and more.
00148996...$16.99

HAL•LEONARD®
www.halleonard.com